IMAGES
of America

HOLLISTON
VOLUME II

IMAGES
of America

HOLLISTON
VOLUME II

Holliston Historical Society

ARCADIA
PUBLISHING

Published by Arcadia Publishing
Charleston, South Carolina

Library of Congress Catalog Card Number: 99-62765

For all general information contact Arcadia Publishing at:
Telephone 843-853-2070
Fax 843-853-0044
E-mail sales@arcadiapublishing.com
For customer service and orders:
Toll-Free 1-888-313-2665

Visit us on the Internet at www.arcadiapublishing.com

CONTENTS

In 1927, Robert Peters used a pinhole camera to catch the view from his house at 230 Washington Street. The building at the far right was Holliston's poor farm.

INTRODUCTION

When Holliston saw the light of day on January 1, 1900, the trolley cars were running along Washington Street, and train service to Boston was frequent and cheap. The first automobiles made their debut around the roads of the town, scaring the horses that still reigned supreme on the roads. George R. Russell took over Charles Morse's store on Central Street. Temperance was a big issue, while voters decided whether or not liquor should be sold in town. Andrew J. Cass kept an eye on the town treasury as if it were his own money, and a lot of it was. The warrant at the town meeting on March 5, 1900, contained 32 articles, including those amounting to $7,600 for the operation of the schools, and $20 for the purchase of grave markers for the town's Revolutionary War soldiers. They also voted to pay each fireman $20 a year for their services. There were 559 students enrolled in school, and Holliston's population was hovering around 3,000.

The shoe shops still provided most employment, and straw hats were rapidly going out of style, so Mowry's factory on Elm Street was going bust. The Andrews block, burned in 1898, had risen from the ashes as a new building with Fiske's store. Change was on the horizon, although no one could have imagined what would take place over the next 50 years.

In 1950, the annual town meeting, March 10, also dealt with financial matters. The School Department was granted $94,600, along with $1,400, for "outside tuition." The Police Department was granted $8,000 for its annual budget. Article 29 on the warrant established a planning board, and they granted $225 to purchase an adding machine for the town officers. There were 654 pupils enrolled in the school system.

Arthur A. Williams was the major employer of shoe workers in Holliston, as the Goodwill Shoe Company still operated on Water Street. Other industries involving machine parts and early electronic components also appeared in shops around Holliston. Valpey Crystal was busy on Highland Street and the Walenar recently opened their shop on Concord Street. The Water Company was finally purchased by the town, and it became the Water Department by 1945.

As the twentieth century loomed to a close, new issues, and a few old ones, were of the utmost concern to Holliston's residents. A town sewerage system is being planned, an idea that was first mentioned 100 years ago. The school budget is spoken of in terms of many millions of dollars, and a new elementary school, the Placentino School, was constructed on Woodland Street. Total school enrollment in 1999 is 3,157, and Holliston's population exceeds 13,000. The Goodwill Shoe Company is no longer here, but its name remains bequeathed to a park on Green Street. The changes have been rapid over the past 100 years, and *Holliston, Volume II* endeavors to chronicle some of those transformations.

Around the time *Holliston, Volume I* was completed, suggestions began to float around about compiling a second volume. After all, most of the pictures in the first edition showed Holliston during the nineteenth century. Here we are at the very end of the twentieth century, a time when camera lenses have been trained on every landscape from below and high, and film has been developed faster than the scenes changed. Many pictures were set aside with the hope of bringing them together in a second collection for Holliston. Along the way, many more pictures were discovered.

Help and contributions came from several people. First, there was the photographic collection bequeathed to the Holliston Historical Society by the estate of Robert H. Peters, a commercial photographer who lived in East Holliston. Peters compiled a large archive of photographs and negatives, recording the major changes in the landscape of Holliston during a pivotal time in the town's history, the mid-twentieth century, when Holliston evolved from a rural community into a suburban town. Many of his pictures were aerial photographs, a concept only imagined 100 years ago. Robert Peters also maintained an extensive archive of reprints of old photographs; he also spent a great deal of time and effort preserving photographs for the Historical Society. Without his work, many of the pictures in the first edition could not have been preserved. A large number of his photographs were initially locked up in old negatives, in sizes that caused many a developer to cringe, since they were not of standard sizes. Robert Peters has left a valuable gift to the people of Holliston, and as a tribute to the work he did so quietly behind the scenes, this second volume is dedicated to his memory.

Sincere thanks and a great deal of gratitude go to John Shannahan, who provided the knowledge and developing equipment needed to bring many of the pictures to life again. Much of what had been started by Mr. Peters was brought to fruition with the assistance of Mr. Shannahan. As word got around, photographs came from other sources. Michael Rossini contributed many of the pictures from the Rossini family's collection. One of their photographs graces the cover of this volume. Ma Rossini is unforgettable, as was Walter's Dairy, and none other than these true icons of Holliston history could be placed upon the cover of this book.

Also, contributions came from Mary Greendale, David Burke, and Paul Guidi. I thank all of them for their efforts in finding truly unique and valuable photographs for this second volume. I have a suspicion that there are many more pictures out there somewhere that could make another great collection. Who knows, perhaps there is a third volume in our future.

–*Joanne Hulbert*

Robert H. Peters

One

DOWNTOWN HOLLISTON

Bird's-eye views of Holliston entered a new phase in the twentieth century, affording viewers a panorama of wonderful sights. Robert Peters accompanied a pilot in August 1949, and took the photograph of Holliston from high above Powder House Hill. Goodwill Park is just below and the apple trees of Hulbert Orchards are in the far distance.

A view of Washington Street in the early 1890s, before the trolley tracks appeared, gives only a hint of the future, except the traffic seems to be increasing downtown.

This photograph was rescued from an 1890s glass negative. Despite the cracks, there is a good view of the old water trough, providing refreshment for man and beast, located curbside in front of Town Hall.

A view of Washington Street from near the corner of Charles Street shows the canopy of trees shading the road. The picture was taken *c.* 1900, since the trolley tracks, placed in 1896, are visible on the right side of the street. The drinking fountain is pictured in its original spot in the middle of the Hollis Street intersection. Imagine trying to get a drink of water if it were still located there.

The trolley is making a stop in the town square just after 1900. Washington Street was unpaved, still marked by the wheels of horse-drawn hacks and wagons, and automobiles had not yet made an appearance.

In 1903, Holliston held a celebration called Old Home Week. Dignitaries made speeches and a great parade passed by a brightly festooned town square. Stephen S. Nichols, one of Holliston's shoe manufacturers, is seen driving his carriage along the parade route.

The Homecoming Parade of 1918 celebrated the return of Holliston's soldiers from World War I. Here the troops pass by Jimmy Inches's store at the Odd Fellows block.

The old brick Andrews block, lost in the fire of 1898, was promptly replaced by a clapboard structure in 1900, and heralded the arrival of the first plate-glass window in Holliston, hidden here by an awning.

The Andrews block is pictured from the south on Washington Street. A crowd of foot traffic on the sidewalk, a wagon along the road, and the trolley tracks help date the photograph taken c. 1900.

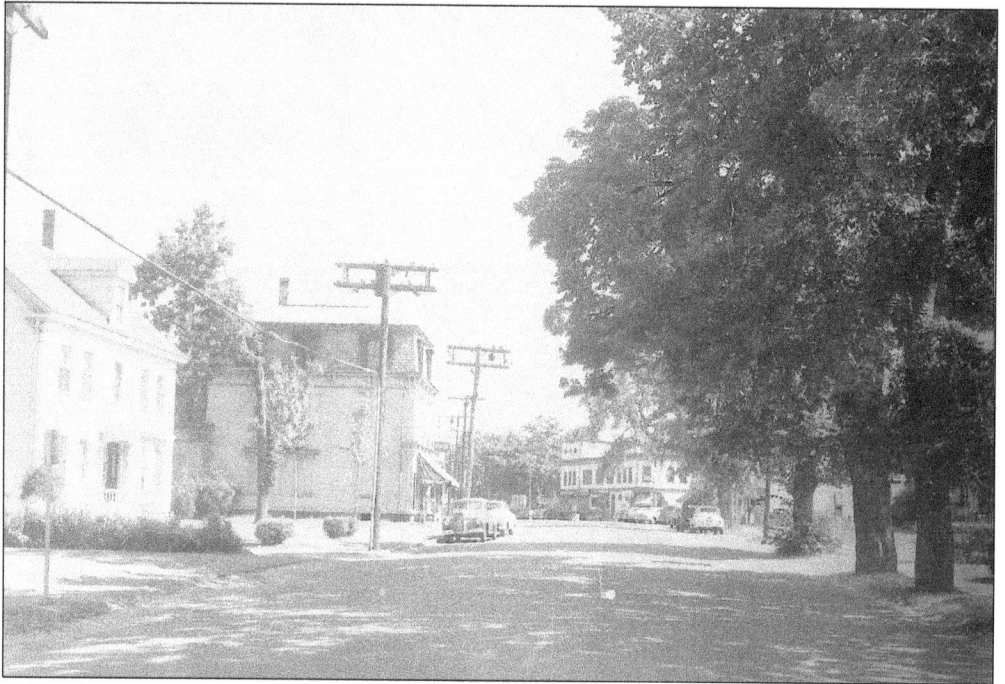

When half of a century passed by, the view on Washington Street gradually changed. There were a few vestiges of the past left. The old Hollis Hotel remained, but many of the stately shade trees had disappeared due to hurricanes and the encroachment of Dutch elm disease.

The old Hollis Hotel had seen better times. Long before this 1955 photograph was taken, the building was part of Holliston's downtown business district. With rooms to let upstairs and storefronts on the ground floor, Al's Restaurant occupied the premises until the shop-worn edifice was razed a few years later.

14

Small changes have occurred since this 1955 photograph of Holliston's business district was taken. The Gulf station is still here, and the store blocks are all recognizable. Only the names are different and some of the stores have changed hands.

As one stepped out of the library and into the middle of Washington Street in August 1955, Holliston's downtown business blocks were in full bloom, and traffic was gradually increasing.

Pond's Block was occupied by several businesses during the 1950s. Williams Market reigned supreme on the corner of Central Street, with Charlie Williams as proprietor. Pete's Restaurant is still right where we expect to find it, and MacKeen's Drugstore stood at the opposite end of the block by Exchange Street.

Edgar Reemie operated his drugstore at the corner of Washington and Central Streets from 1907 to 1955. Reemie dispensed more than 85,000 prescriptions during those years, and was available nights and weekends for emergency medications. MacKeen operated his drugstore at the corner of Washington and Exchange Streets since 1925, and was the youngest pharmacist to own a store in Massachusetts at that time. He moved his store to Reemie's location at the Central Street corner in 1955.

16

In 1955, the former Andrews Block was known as the Cerel Building. Fiske's was still there, half its present size, and the First National Store occupied the east side of the present store. Aubuchon's hardware store was also located there. Chief Holbrook's cruiser can be seen parked curbside.

By 1963, Aubuchon's was still located in the Cerel Building, and Fiske's Store had become R.J. Moore Inc. The transformation was brief, as the Fiske name eventually returned to the sign over the door, where it will witness another turn of a century.

Annie Fiske took over the store her father, James F. Fiske, started. Her name was indelibly tied to the enterprise for most of the twentieth century, and the store was popularly known as "Annie Fiske's" for long after her passing in 1953.

Ted Loring still manned the cash register at Fiske's on April 23, 1956, his 80th birthday.

The Odd Fellows Block, seen here in 1955, housed Knowlton's Market and Jimmy Inches's store at the opposite end.

The Nissen's truck made deliveries to Knowlton's, and a truck still makes a stop there at the Superette today. The Edison store is now gone, and Jimmy Inches has been replaced by Dee Robbins's hair salon.

In 1956, changes were made to the facade of the Odd Fellows Block, an attempt to "modernize" the appearance of the building. Evidence of the facelift is still visible today. The Holliston Superette now reigns supreme where Batchelder and Knowlton once supplied groceries.

At the Holliston Superette we . . .
Do not make a stingy sandwich,
We pile the cold cuts high,
Customers like to see Salami,
Comin' through the rye . . .

—Anonymous, 1999

The Holliston Public Library opened in 1904. Built with money donated in part from Andrew Carnegie and from its citizens, Holliston's literary oasis is seen here in a photograph taken in 1940.

Yesterday Aloise Maeder placed in the entrance to the new library building, under one of the pillars, a jar containing a recent town report, assessor's valuation report, poll tax list, list of savings bank officers, names of the building committee, name of the architect, name of the contractor, amount of the gift to the library construction by Andrew Carnegie and a copy of each Boston, Milford and Holliston newspapers. (December 22, 1903)

The Town Hall, in this 1949 photograph, shows little change from pictures taken 50 years later. The old war memorial and honor roll stands in front of the building, soon replaced by the present granite monument; the front steps have been restored to the wide wooden planks of a past era.

Photographs of Mudville are rare indeed. School Street looked like a small country path in this *c.* 1900 picture.

Two

ALONG CENTRAL STREET

The disastrous Andrew Block fire of December 28, 1898, also destroyed commercial buildings on Central Street. Such a calamity called for photographic mementos to be published and widely distributed as a remembrance of the event.

Modern times have afforded a greater birds-eye view of the landscape of Holliston. Shown here are the following: the area of Central Street with the railroad line and depot (bottom right),

Goodwill Shoe (left), and the farm known as Linda Vista, an expanse of fields in 1949, and now occupied by Marked Tree Road. (upper left).

Central Street, seen here in August 1955, was flanked by Charlie Williams's market at Pond's Block and the Cerel Building on the opposite corner, forming a gateway to another of Holliston's commercial areas.

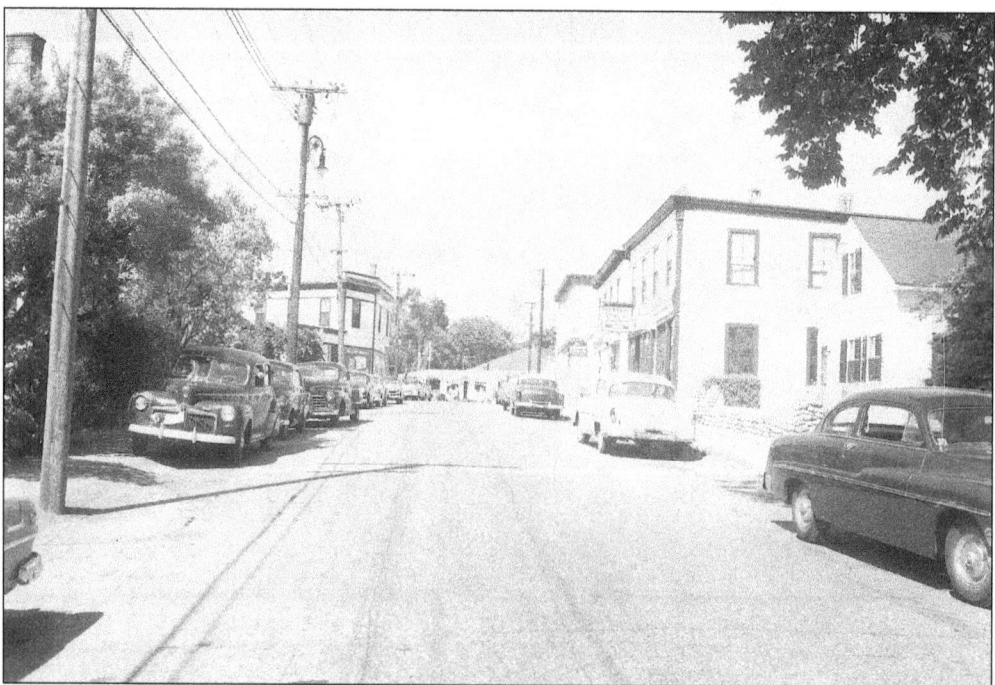

Parking appears to have been a perennial problem even in 1955, as cars squeezed along both sides of the street, right up onto the sidewalks.

In 1963, the very popular and memorable Yellow Door Gift Shop occupied a store on Central Street, offering small gifts, crafts, cards, and jewelry. The Betti family operated a shoe store in the block next door.

Again, the landscape along Central Street experienced major changes, as the store block was torn down, making way for a parking area, perhaps alleviating some of the congestion along the street.

More space was needed for a post office building in Holliston, and a site on Central Street was chosen in 1955. A house and a vacant lot were sacrificed for the accommodation. Ah, such a centralized, downtown convenience, too!

Maeder Row was transformed from a verdant lane to a major side street. At one time, as seen in 1955, there were more weeds than asphalt.

Central Street continued-on with a few more familiar sights in 1955. The Esso station occupied a garage next to the fire station, and a barbershop was located beside the brook.

Joe Larosa stands proudly by his new barbershop on Central Street in 1955.

The old Russell's market was razed to make room for the new "modernized" supermarket of the twentieth century, forcing another relic of old times to come crashing down in a heap of rubble. The new store peeks out from behind the old, doomed edifice.

The "new" Russell's was ready for service in 1959. Gone were the old barrels and bins, the creaking wooden floor, and the old ice chests. Instead, the town was now treated to the newer, faster cash registers, cellophane-wrapped food in convenient containers, piped-in music, doors that opened for you, and a smooth and silent linoleum floor. Ah, progress!

Three

EAST HOLLISTON

The Gates brothers, Clarence and Bert, owned a gas station and Hudson car dealership in the old trolley barn at East Holliston, on Washington Street, by Houghton's Pond. The pump dispensed Indian gas at the time and in later years offered Texaco. The Gates name remains a part of East Holliston, as the fire station, located just behind their old building, was named in honor of Clarence Gates.

An aerial view of the East Holliston corner, taken in 1949, reveals a small village with sweeping stretches of open space. Houghton's Pond is in the foreground, Mill Pond and the arched

bridge are to the left, and something appears to be burning over by the Shawmut Waxed Paper Company on Railroad Street.

Another aerial view, also taken in 1949, looking to the north over the East Holliston corner,

shows forest and fields, where houses and commercial buildings would later bloom.

A 1980 photograph of the East Holliston corner shows the traffic light, so familiar to Hollistonians today, but the streetscape has changed. The building that housed Costa's store is to the right, the old Houghton house behind the Mobil station was ready for demolition, and the little brick building has disappeared.

Clarence and Bert Gates lived in the house at the East Holliston corner. They were around to see the traffic change from wagons to cars, and witnessed the installment of the traffic light. They also witnessed the Ted Williams's fender-bender in August 1946. Perhaps Ted would have appreciated it if the light had been put up sooner. May you ponder that the next time you are waiting for the light to change.

36

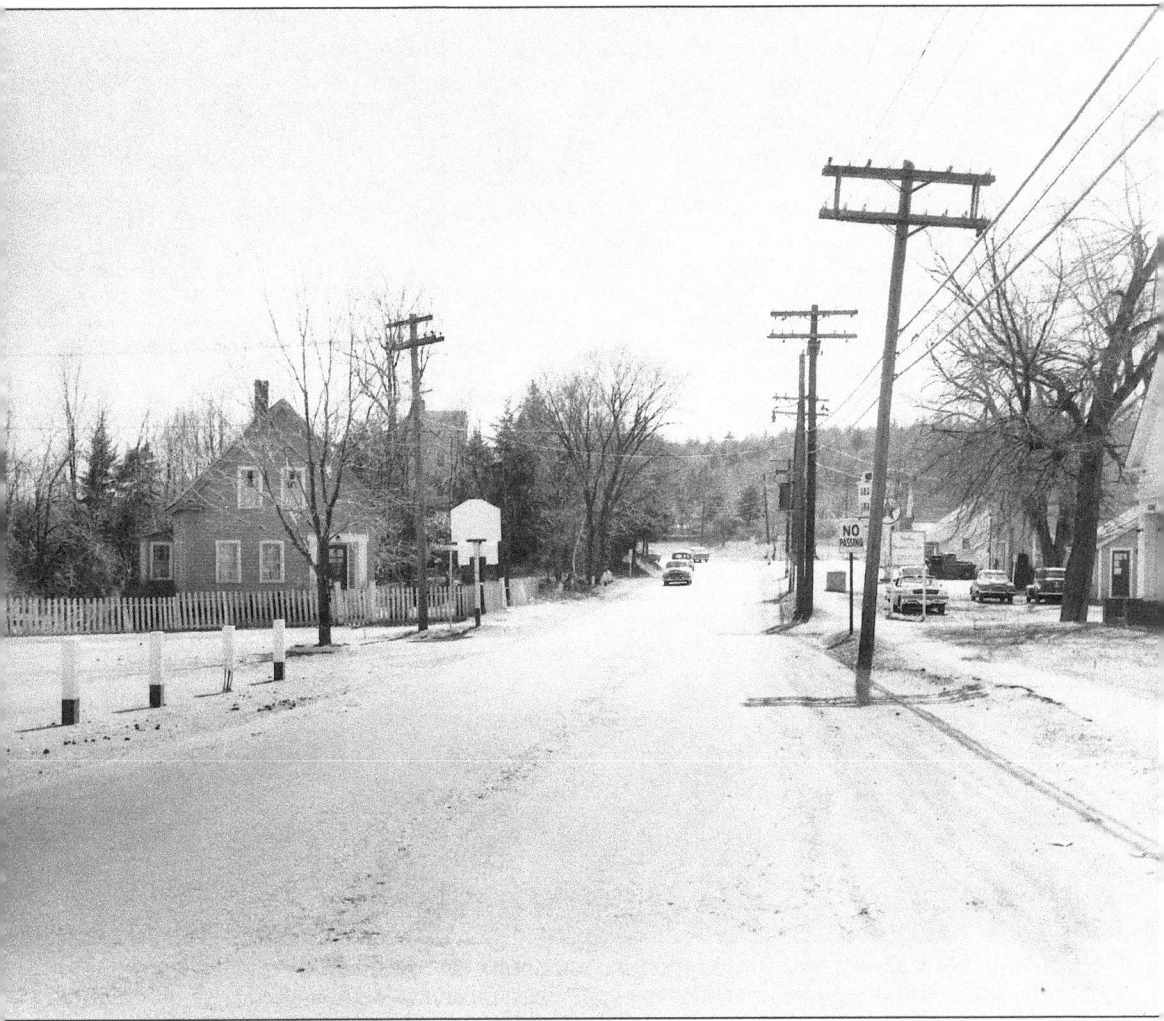

Washington Street has always been an important commercial center of the town. Factories were built there to take advantage of the waterpower supplied by Jarr Brook and Houghton's Pond, and although the types of industry have changed, the east village has remained an important business center. The 1959 photograph reflects the gradual changes that have transformed this section of town. Here are fleeting glimpses of Tito Rossini's "Country Store," the Gates's garage, and the Morley Equipment Company, as well as a house now gone, torn down to make more room for commercial buildings.

37

Caleb Stevens was a genial man even if he was not reckoned a financier among the townsfolk. His home and store were located at the house with pillars on Washington Street, just beyond Curve Street. It was fortunate that making straw hats was a flourishing home industry then. He closed his store in debt, and would have lost the home but that his wife took in straw to sew into hats and earned the money to pay the bills. His house has stood the test of time. Here the house is seen decorated for Christmas in 1955.

East Holliston boasted of many prosperous businesses in the 1800s. There were four successive owners to the building on Washington Street at the corner of Baker Street. Lovett Fiske opened a grocery business, and, after several years, Mr. Fiske sold out to Luther and Lewis Turner. Later they decided to follow Horace Greeley's advice to "Go west, young man" and moved to Chicago. The store was then taken over by Jackson Parmenter, who did a brisk business of selling wood shavings by the barrel load. In more recent times, the building became the office of Dr. Bernard Lubke.

Deacon Timothy Daniels was an outstanding merchant and citizen of Holliston during the nineteenth century. His store in East Holliston on Washington Street, the second house beyond Baker Street, included a tailor shop. This store and another on Cat Hill, or Metcalf as it is now known, were probably the only two in town *c.* 1840.

Seen here in a picture taken in 1980, the old Town Farm, located at 245 Washington Street, housed Holliston's sick or indigent residents from 1892 to *c.* 1940, when the local welfare system adopted modern trends. Before 1892, Holliston's poor traveled to the town of Ashland to a farm caught within that new town's boundaries in 1846, when a large portion of Holliston was ceded to the new town.

During the 1970s, the old Moses Harriman house became the new home of the Holliston Pediatric Group. Seen here in 1981, thousands of children from Holliston and the surrounding towns have found medical care here, first from Drs. Fisch and Starobin, and also from many other physicians and nurses who came here to work with them.

Robert Peters's home was located at 230 Washington Street. Hidden by a thick cover of trees, the house was rarely seen by passersby, as only the winding driveway gave evidence of its existence. The house is gone now, along with the extensive beehive that lived within its walls; the houses of Quail Run now occupy the acreage.

October 31, 1958, marked the end of an era, as the East Holliston Post Office, located at the train station along Washington Street, closed its doors forever. Here, Postmistress Frances Danforth receives the last mailbag into the station and passes along to Joe Damigella the last outgoing bag of mail.

Mrs. Danforth sorts out the last of the mail for the East Holliston residents who maintained their mailboxes at the station. Railroad service to the station was also cut back, so no longer did a passenger get off the train, pick up his/her mail, and then walk home. Modern amenities such as the automobile had made such "conveniences" obsolete.

The pot-bellied stove held court in the middle of the lobby, providing heat for postal patrons, train passengers, and the regular crowd that lingered at the station to catch up on local news and make social calls.

Postmistress Danforth closes up for the last time. Robert Peters accompanied her on her last appointed rounds. He reported, "Mrs. Hedberg was the last one in before 3:20 p.m., when I took Mrs. D. to Parker Products, Pfeiffers, and Ed Serocki's. Then we returned and John Snyder was the last one in before the official closing at 3:45 . . ."

Lowland Street is seen in 1932, from the roof of the barn at Hulbert Orchards. One of the few expanses of acreage in town relatively free of rock, the land was rich with high-grade sand. The excavations in the foreground show evidence of the trainloads of the sand that

were periodically shipped to New York State for use in cider filtering. The apple orchard was started in 1926, and continued until 1954, when the majority of the trees were destroyed by two hurricanes.

Robert Peters took to the air again and photographed the orchards and the cranberry bogs beyond, all located near Mill Pond and the arched bridge. His house is hidden in the thick cluster of trees in the foreground. Lake Winthrop looms in the hazy distance.

At ground level, the apple orchard in winter is pictured in a view looking from near where Norland and Regal Streets meet, and the old barn and house at 100 Woodland Street are seen in the distance.

Robert Peters caught one last photograph of the old frog pond at Hulbert Orchards on Valentine's Day, 1956. The location is now filled with the houses of Norland Street. Perhaps the spot was near and dear to his heart since he could see the pond from his house. Soon after, the view from his window was quite different.

Yet till the world's imperious command
Scattered us widely up and down the land,
Man-grown, we sought the Pond in Winter, Spring,
Summer, Autumn, never wearying,
And ever, when returning to those haunts,
Whether gay June her sumptuous beauty flaunts,
Or grim December boasts his ice—as then,
We swim or skate, and dream we're boys again.

"The Pond,"
—William Addison Houghton, 1911

The arched bridge on Woodland Street has been a local landmark since its construction in 1847. Holliston residents are lucky that the Boston and Worcester Railroad decided to build such a beautiful bridge instead of just filling in the gap, as they did elsewhere along the track. Repairs to the bridge were made in 1920, when the cement edging was added along the top edge and the bridge spanning Boggastow Brook was modernized.

Four

WALTER'S DAIRY

During the spring of 1940, a small building was put up at the corner of Concord and Washington Streets in East Holliston. At the time it seemed like an ambitious project on the part of the Rossini family. The whole family worked hard, the food was good, and the ice cream was excellent. Built by local carpenters, George Mantell and Weldon Gwynn, the original building was a humble size, but foretold of greater things to come.

The name of Rossini has been around Holliston for quite a while. In the beginning, there were two brothers, Tito and Joseph, who came from Italy c. 1900. Joseph's four sons, Walter, John, Alex, and Beno, seen here with "Ma" Rossini in a photograph taken in 1940, opened the stand that specialized in ice cream and hot dogs, becoming Holliston's first drive-up, of sorts.

The original ice cream stand was functional but a little cramped. Ice cream cones cost 10¢, and frappes were 25¢. French fries were then available at 20¢ for the small order, 50¢ for the large. Sonny Rossini is seen here manning the counter.

Working at Walter's Dairy was a prized memory for a generation of Holliston's youths. The youthful employees would occasionally change, but "Ma" was always there. During World War II, "Ma" carried the effort to keep the dairy open during these four difficult years. In spite of war shortages of every kind, Walter's Dairy never closed.

After World War II, it was obvious to the Rossini brothers, as it had long been to their patrons, that something had to be done immediately to increase the size of the plant. Once again, despite restrictions and shortages, they felt they must add to and re-plan the original building. Those who watched the struggles of this family to get the new building completed eagerly awaited the grand opening on June 24, 1947.

The counter space at the new Walter's Dairy increased dramatically. Booths were added, and the very popular jukebox prepared Holliston for the 1950s in excellent style.

The community of Holliston and people from an increasingly greater distance found this a good place to eat. The photograph was taken in July 1957. While families enjoyed great Italian food in the dining room, the young adults of Holliston were more likely to be found around the soda fountain or outside in the parking lot looking over hot rods.

Walter's Dairy remained a landmark until the 1980s. Bertucci's Restaurant acquired the location and continued to serve Italian food. Still, life was just not the same at the East Holliston corner.

This ice-cutting machine, built by Joe and Tito Rossini from old car and truck parts, was hard at work on Houghton's Pond.

Perhaps it was natural that the Rossini brothers would make and sell ice cream at Walter's Dairy. Joe Rossini is performing a balancing act at the ice-cutting yard, which was operated by the Rossini family on Houghton's Pond during the early decades of the twentieth century.

Joseph Rossini arrived in Holliston c. 1900, and started a business cutting and selling blocks of ice taken from Houghton's Pond.

Though you live a life obscure,
Tranquil happiness it knows,
Joys you have, unfailing, pure,
Joys that honest toil bestows.

from "La Fiorista"
—Antonio Peretti, (translated by William Addison Houghton)

Joseph Rossini is seated upon the ground and his brother, Tito, stands at the left, with the smokestack of the S. Wilder Co. just behind him. Two other relatives join them in this photograph, taken in the backyard of the Rossini residence at East Holliston corner.

Five

AT HOME IN HOLLISTON

Franklin Addison Stone started a shoe factory at the corner of Central and Winthrop Streets in 1860. His house was located around the corner at 115 Norfolk Street. He liked the lot so much that he removed an older house in order to place his house in just the right spot. Stone was involved in town politics and especially liked taking part in liquor raids. His old factory, idle for six months, burned to the ground during the blizzard of 1888.

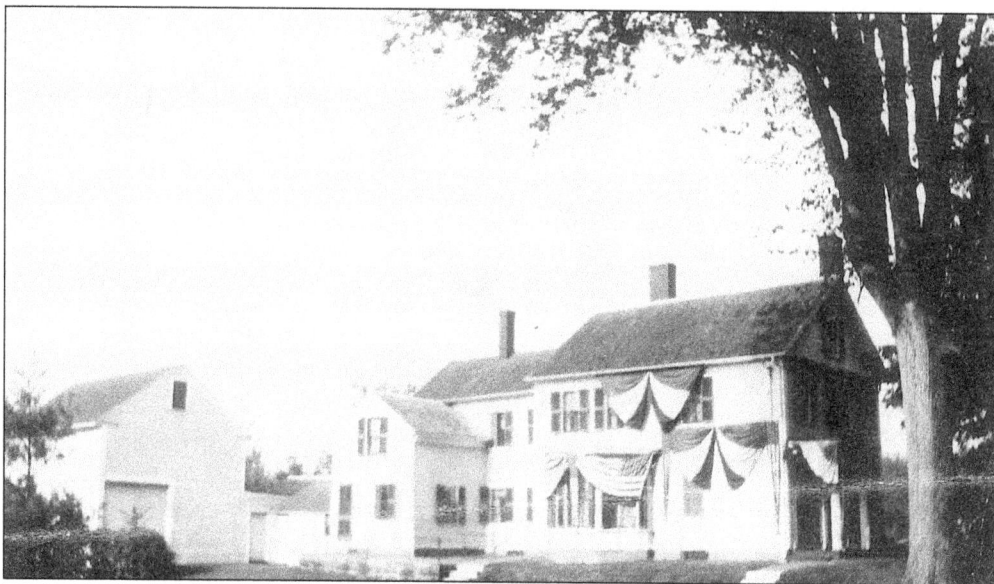

The James F. Fiske house at 20 Hollis Street is decorated for Holliston's 200th anniversary in 1924. Fiske owned the newspaper store in the Andrews Building and held many town offices, most notably, treasurer. His daughter, Annie, took over the store and lived in the family home until her death in May 1953.

One might think there would be more stone houses in Holliston, due to the abundance of stone, but the architectural heritage came from England, where wood prevailed. A few brave souls did erect stone houses. Located on Hollis Street, this rare gem stands as a tribute to the quarrying industry, which supplied a multitude of foundations, walls, and an occasional building.

By 1980, Linda Vista had lost some of the porches and peaks of a bygone era and was beginning to look "more like itself," but the name remained. The house continues to occupy a prominent place on the slope of Phipps Hill on Washington Street.

The house at Dog Corner, most recently honored as the residence of clockmaker John Losch, is located in Holliston at the Milford line on Washington Street.

The Andrew J. Cass house, 1077 Washington Street, is located at the top of Phipps Hill. This prominent man in town politics was dubbed the "Watch Dog of the Town Treasury." He fearlessly spoke his opinions and often won by his eloquence and keen insight on many apparently hopeless issues. Cass died on Christmas Eve in 1902, after being accidentally run over by a trolley car near his home.

Andrew Cass's son, Frank, was a gentleman farmer like his father, and was also well schooled in the fine arts of frugality. Frank was postmaster in Holliston for many years, and a state representative for a few, too.

Frank Cass was not the forceful advocate for frugality his father was. When Andrew died in 1902, Frank acquired much of the real estate on Phipps Hill.

In 1908, Frank built a new house in the field across the street from his father's farm. With opulent, Richardsonian-style architecture, the house at 1090 Washington Street reflected new trends for a new century.

The Benjamin Wiley house at Metcalf is an interesting building, and historian Dan Chase commented extensively about this house. It stands on Washington Street, at the southwest corner of Oak Street. In structure it resembles a Cape Cod cottage, with a great central four-flue chimney. In the cellar is a massive brick cistern, and the chimney is on two brick piers, joined by four-inch oak or chestnut logs, with flat stones on them. Behind the house once stood a huge barn, and to the south of the barnyard stood an old shoe shop. Behind the barn along Oak Street there was a magnificent elm, one of the largest in town. Chase speculated the house was built in the 1830s. Ben Wiley was a Civil War veteran.

Littlefield Tavern, located at 1919 Washington Street, may have been built between 1680 and 1700. Once the center of Tory activity in Holliston, the tavern became the unofficial headquarters of the *Rang de Dangs*, a notoriously undisciplined company of the local militia, after the Revolutionary War. During its heyday the tavern sign pictured a girl milking a cow. This photograph was taken in 1957.

The Littlefield Tavern, as seen in 1980 enveloped in trees and bushes, remains by the side of Washington Street. George Washington and his entourage are said to have stopped here for refreshment while traveling from Cambridge, Massachusetts, to Hartford, Connecticut, and New York, New York, in 1789.

The Elihu Cutler House, at the corner of Washington and Linden Streets, continued to be gradually encroached upon by the ever-widening Washington Street. By 1980, there was no more room to grow.

Another pillared house on Washington Street, near Elm Street, was best known in the twentieth century as the home and office of Dr. William Byrne. Dr. Bernard Lubke took over the practice, as well as the house. Lubke later moved his office to East Holliston.

Seth Thayer built his house in 1860 on Washington Street. After amassing a tidy fortune selling straw hats in Cincinnati, he returned to Holliston, where he opened a country store in the center of town and another near Mill Pond on Woodland Street. He was praised for a $500 donation toward the enhancement of the public library, where a portrait of Thayer now hangs.

Orrin Thompson, born in 1821, came to Holliston from Hubbardston in 1843. He organized the Holliston Savings Bank in 1872, was elected to many town offices, and was involved in town matters regarding bounties and pensions paid out from the Civil War. His home, located at 854 Washington Street, became the location of the Chesmore Funeral Home. This photograph of the house was taken in 1956.

The house located at 100 Woodland Street was built *c.* 1820 by James Wight. The construction time was opportune, because the old meetinghouse was being raised at that time, and this house inherited the granite front step and some of the interior panels from the old building. The photograph was taken in the 1920s, near the time when Albert Shippee sold the property and it became Hulbert Orchards.

The house at 277 Washington Street, seen here in 1981 quietly nestled by the stonewalls near the old poor farm along a busy street, was once the home of Ferdinand Pluta. Born in Warsaw, Poland, March 3, 1810, Pluta, a Polish exile, reached this country at the age of 25, after serving in the war between Russia and Poland. His experience through life had been "wide and varied, intermingled with the severe trials so early in life, of being banished from those he dearly loved, after having been reared in luxury." He married Mary Houghton of Sherborn, raised four children, and worked at the woolen mill on Mill Pond.

New styles of architecture bloomed in the twentieth century. One notable house reflecting a new look was the estate known as Basquaerie Farms on Goulding Street, seen here in 1956. The house was part of a 352-acre farm that included present-day Glen Ellen Country Club, which is located across the town line in Millis. Built in 1940–41, this contemporary home, with 11 rooms designed by Boston architect Robert Louis Stevenson, reflected the demands of the twentieth century with the inclusion of a 3-car garage and a 6-car detached garage.

Other new styles of architecture appeared on the landscape in Holliston. Few were as prevalent as the ranch style home, with one-story and a sometimes rambling layout, which appealed to builders and homeowners alike. The house, pictured here in 1951, is located at 50 Highland Street near the town line with Ashland.

Modern times provided new types of living space. Elderly housing made its debut in Holliston in 1974, with the construction of Cole Court at 492 Washington Street. Here, the site was well on its way to completion in July of that year.

The housing complex was completed, and this picture was taken in June 1975, showing the start of a new neighborhood in Holliston. These new types of living space are appreciated by a large number of longtime Holliston residents.

Six

SCHOOL DAYS

Looking the part of the lean, mean ice machine are the players of the Holliston High School Ice Hockey Team for the years 1926–1927. Games were played on Lake Winthrop as long as the weather cooperated and opponents could be found. The high school hockey team began playing organized games as early as 1918.

The old Walker High School was located on Hollis Street, just behind the town hall and the Congregational church. The school was named for Principal George F. Walker, who helped organize the public high school when the Mount Hollis Academy closed its doors in 1851.

The large wooden building served as a high school until 1957, when the town's population demanded larger quarters. The picture was taken in 1955, when students were still wandering the halls. The old academic relic was unceremoniously torn down in 1958.

The Holliston High School Class of 1942 appear hopeful, optimistic, and bright. Superintendent of Schools Fred Miller wrote the following in the Town Annual Report: "Over 50% of all pupils in grades 7 through 12 are engaged in some form of necessary war victory work. Their schoolwork is affected, but this loss is unavoidable under total war conditions." Some of the graduates went to college; Miller also reported that several boys had left school to enlist or to work full time.

May Dance (1952) at the upper town hall was a big event of the high school year. The band played on stage, there was dancing, and the maypole, too. The ever-present chaperones sit attentively on the sidelines.

The year was 1952. The play was performed onstage at the upper town hall. The name of the play is unknown, but the costumes are truly inspiring.

The Cutler School, as seen in 1955, was the first school in Holliston in the 1890s to consolidate each grade level into its own classroom, instead of mixing classes like the outlying schoolhouses. At first, there were protests from parents reluctant to send their children all the way downtown on school barges driven by strangers. Eventually, everyone adjusted to the new system.

Flagg School, as seen in 1955, brought a new look to schools in Holliston with its one-story architecture, a gymnasium, and an excellent baseball diamond next door on Linden Street.

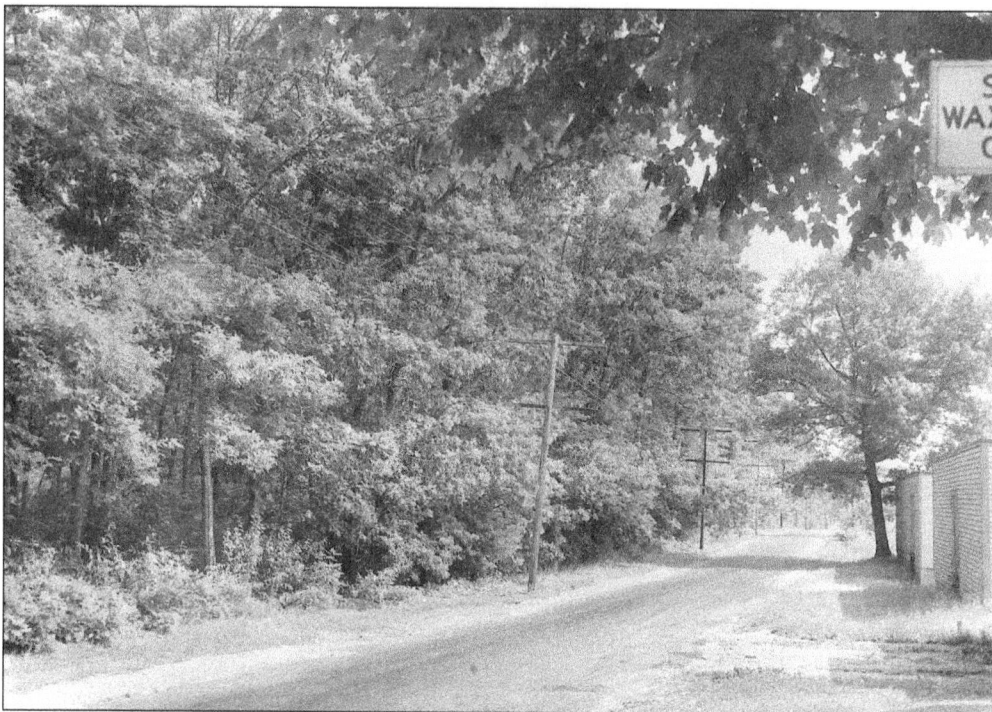

The view along Woodland Street before construction began on a new high school building shows a road along the thick forest of oak trees that covered the area. A few of the trees remain today. Only the Flagg School and the Shawmut Waxed Paper Company were around before new neighbors moved in.

The construction on the "new" high school building began in 1956. No longer would the basketball team have to play games at the town hall. There was an auditorium, too, as well as many more classrooms, a shop, a music room, and even a football field!

Construction continued into 1957. The facility was ready for its first class in September 1957, and the Class of 1958 was the first to leave these new, hallowed halls.

A third generation of the Holliston High School soon followed. An even-larger building was needed by the 1970s, and a new facility was built on Hollis Street in one of the Finn Farm's fields. Today, the school building is holding its own, with no plans on the horizon to move to a fourth building.

The Andrews School, seen in 1908, is the third building to stand upon this spot. Once known as Schoolhouse Number Eight, it was the beloved alma mater of generations of Holliston's students. Still bearing the name of Thomas E. Andrews, a prominent Holliston businessman and banker of more than a century ago, the building no longer welcomed students into its classrooms in 1998. The building was "retired" by the school system.

The Wilder School, seen here in 1980, was one of the last outposts of the old school system. The second building to occupy this site, the location was quaint, quiet, and isolated from the other school buildings. The school was more recently dubbed "L'Ecole Wilder" as part of the French immersion program.

76

The school activities in Holliston were varied and unique. Cutler School students parade along Washington Street in April 1950, in what was called the "Circus Parade." There was no circus coming to town, but imagination goes a long way.

Sports have played a big part in Holliston's school history. The boys began playing basketball near the turn of the century, and the game was a main attraction in town during each winter season. The 1928–29 high school team included the legendary Charles Wonoski (back row, second from left), a player who went on to a brief moment of fame playing professional baseball in England.

Holliston High School still fielded strong basketball teams in 1951, where they still played at town hall. The teams were larger, and the write-ups in local sports columns continued to praise their skill. The coach (left, standing) is none other than Ray Tondorf, a local sports legend, whose name is still linked with local baseball teams with the Tondorf League.

The boys were not outdone by the girls on the playing field, as seen in this portrait of the 1941–42 high school team. Basketball was first played by women in Holliston on March 15, 1907. The press reviews that day were not kind to the girls, for they "created a furor with their picturesque costumes and labored gyrations in chasing the elusive sphere." They survived the ordeal and reportedly did well for beginners.

Later years saw more success in team sports for women. Basketball was still going strong in 1952. The sport would prove to be one of the most successful athletic programs for women at Holliston High School.

Sports carried on even during summer vacation. The Holliston Flyers baseball team was part of the Tri-County League and played opposing teams from nearby towns. This team picture was prompted by the non-league game played against a team of fathers and uncles on August 9, 1953. The boys won easily.

Seven

INDUSTRY

When 1900 rolled around, boots and shoes were still manufactured in Holliston, although the glory days had certainly passed. This 1890s photograph is a portrait of the aging industry that followed Holliston's future into a new century. The Batchelder brothers had all passed on. Richard Feelehey still kept busy over on Winthrop Street, but his days were numbered. John Clancy, not wanting to be the last of the shoe manufacturers in Holliston, looked for a successor as he saw himself approaching retirement; he did not want to leave the many shoe workers without employment.

In 1908, John Clancy asked Arthur A. Williams of Cochituate, owner of the Goodwill Shoe Company, to relocate to Holliston, where there was a vacant factory, built on Water Street in 1891. After an unfortunate fire at his factory in Cochituate, Williams formed the Safety First Shoe Company in Holliston in 1910.

Williams soon expanded his factory complex and constructed an additional building on the west side of Water Street. In 1928 the Safety First Shoe Company was the only producer of steel-toe footwear in New England, and in 1939 was the third largest producer in the United States.

Much has been speculated about the tunnel under Water Street that connects the two buildings. Williams said the hidden passageway was to protect raw materials being delivered from the storeroom of the stock building to the factory. Finished footwear, all packed in cartons on the fourth floor of the factory, was returned to the storeroom by overhead cable car. Others believed that Williams wanted to keep his trade secrets hidden from public view.

Arthur A. Williams, his wife, and son stand proudly by his exhibition boot, the advertising symbol of the Safety First Shoe Company. The boot stands 7 feet, 6 inches tall; measures 5 feet, 4 inches from heel to toe; and is actually a perfect size 168. The built-in steel toe, first offered in 1925, by the Safety First Shoe Company, guaranteed protection of the workman's foot from heavy objects, molten metals, and even a snake bite.

This is an aerial picture of Water Street at the Goodwill Shoe Company and Safety First Shoe Company, August 1949. The large factory building on the west side of the railroad, on

Exchange Street, was the Berkshire Shoe Company. It is known as the first company to produce the well-known footwear classic, the Saddle Shoe.

The Shawmut Waxed Paper Company was located at Railroad and Woodland Streets near the intersection of Linden Street. The company manufactured waxed paper wrappers, mainly for the bakery industry, and were similar to those seen today on specialty breads. Arthur W. Moore brought his company to Holliston in 1906. Shawmut was the only producer of wax paper wrappers in Massachusetts at that time. Besides being an astute businessman, Moore also possessed a creative and innovative mind. He obtained a patent for his waxed paper cutter box just in time for Christmas in 1940.

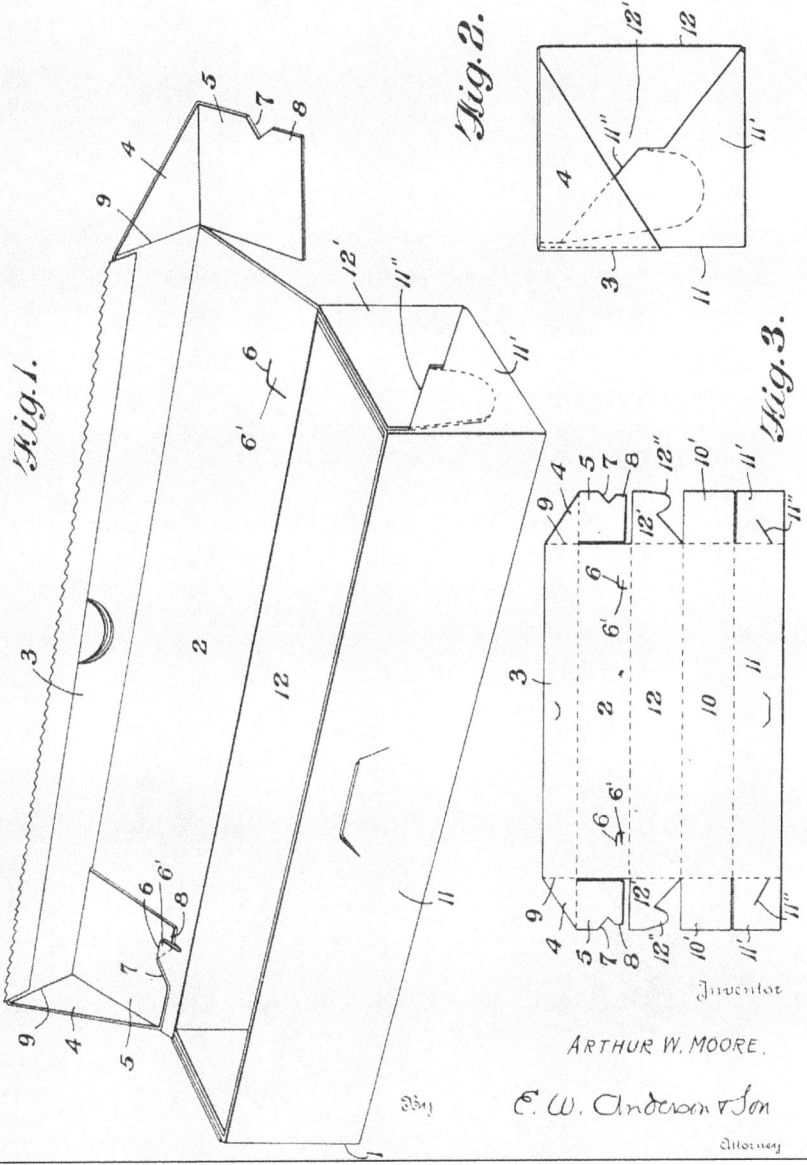

Fig.1.

Fig.2.

Fig.3.

Inventor

ARTHUR W. MOORE.

E. W. Anderson & Son

Attorney

This is a blueprint of Arthur W. Moore's 1940 patented waxed paper cutter box.

87

Walenar Manufacturing Company was located at 551 Concord Street. A precision machine shop that made delicate and intricate parts for many industries, the company was founded in 1944, by Walter Partington, Leonard Snow, and Arthur Champney. Each contributed, in addition to know-how and funds, letters from their first names to form the company name. One notable product was a metal piece the size of a fist, with 176 dimensions, that was used in Raytheon's Sparrow missile project of the 1960s. The company photograph was taken in June 1950.

Century Manufacturing Company, located at 383 Fiske Street, specialized in metal stampings and the manufacture of tiny metal clamps, switches, and terminals used as electronic contacts in the automotive and other industries. The company was started in 1950 and has been in continuous production for a half century.

ChildLife, Inc. was founded in 1945 by Arnold White. While seeking a safe alternative to heavy wooden swing seats, which were notorious for causing injuries to children, Mr. White made soft, flexible swings for his own children from old-fashioned industrial conveyor belting. Soon he devised other play equipment, such as climbers, slides, tree houses, mountain climbing walls, and swing sets. ChildLife equipment has been featured on the *Today Show*, the *Cosby Show*, and *This Old House*, as well as on the grounds of the White House.

Each year, ChildLife published a catalog, and many of Holliston's nursery, kindergarten, and grade schoolchildren were seen as major models for the brochures. Stars of the 1950 catalog, taken in August 1949, appear in this photograph.

Holliston Sand Company was located on Lowland Street and produced high-grade, silicon-rich sand used in glass-making. Like very fine beach sand, the unique grade is found in rare pockets around New England. Finding this sand dune of sorts is one of Holliston's more interesting geological features. This 1954 photograph was taken during the height of activity at the location. Sand was conveyed through the long cylindrical kiln (right), as the glow of the fire and the rumble of the engines powering it could be seen and heard well into the night for a mile around.

Eight

HOUSES OF WORSHIP

The front entrance to the First Congregational Church, November 1949, shows a church now painted white, a new wrought-iron handrail, and the southeast-facing granite steps, warmed by the early rising sun. In 1877, Reverend Adams echoed the sentiment of his predecessor, Reverend Dickinson, who had, in 1800, also voiced his concern for the throngs of young adults that congregated nightly upon the meetinghouse steps. The arrival of Walter's Dairy was many decades off in the future.

A 1956 photograph reveals a scene still familiar today: the recently added Jordan Hall and the old high school building looming above on the hill.

The parsonage of the Congregational Church had been located at various places over the years. In 1916, the house at 674 Washington Street was occupied by the minister and his family.

NEAR·THIS·SPOT·STOOD
THE·FIRST·MEETINGHOUSE
IN·HOLLISTON
BUILT·IN·1725   TAKEN·DOWN·IN·1823
THIS·MEMORIAL
WAS·ERECTED·BY·THE·FIRST·CONGREGATIONAL·CHURCH
1909

A bronze plaque marks the location of the first meetinghouse in Holliston. Located near the corner of Washington Street, near the entrance-way between the United Church of Christ and the Town Hall, the building would have stood where the westbound lane of Washington Street is today. Instead, the building was partially torn down, parts were scattered around town, and the remaining building served as the early town house until the present town hall was built in the 1850s.

The original Baptist church was an impressive edifice. Located at the corner of Washington and Charles Streets, the building was an attractive, wooden Gothic structure, painted in a multitude of colors and decorated with stained-glass windows.

Disaster struck in September 1938, when the famous hurricane rampaged through Holliston. The Baptist church suffered the most damage of any building in town.

A smaller building was soon placed upon the site in 1940, where the grand old edifice once stood. The Great Depression years and World War II did not allow for the construction of such grand buildings as was possible in the 1870s. The photograph was taken in 1959.

Years passed, and better economic times arrived. The church membership grew, and a need for a larger building became apparent by 1962. A field located on High Street, just behind Gardner Morse's residence, became the site for a new church building.

This 1971 photograph of the "new" Baptist church shows the A-frame design. A popular style in the 1960s, the A-frame was adopted, appropriately, by churches, to provide an open sanctuary with easy accommodation of a growing church membership.

St. Michael's Episcopal Church, located on Highland Street, was also an A-frame building. The church became St. Michael's permanent home in 1971, after many years of temporary quarters in Holliston.

Christ the King Lutheran Church built their sanctuary on Central Street in 1968, and it was the first Lutheran church in Holliston.

St. Mary's Church is another fine example of wooden Gothic architecture. The building was started in 1870, and 12 years later, was completed enough for Mass to be held in the main sanctuary. This photograph dates to the 1980s.

There have been recent changes to the exterior of St. Mary's, and there have been many significant renovations to the interior over the nearly 130 years of the church. A wedding in November 1951 shows the interior, which was quite different from today.

The Xavarian Brothers Seminary, established in 1949, is located on Summer Street. Young men from around the world were outfitted for missionary work. They carried the Word of God to missions throughout the world, to many people, who also became familiar with that town far away in America—Holliston. Very active in the 1950s, the chapel and gardens of the Fatima Shrine still attract visitors from all around New England.

On the grounds of the Fatima Shrine is the largest rosary in the world, constructed in 1965. Each stone bears a plaque with the words of the rosary in a different language.

A truly rare glimpse of a religious treasure in Holliston is the first synagogue. At the dedication of the sanctuary, Rabbi Shoher said, "We should be grateful to Almighty God that this country is an asylum for the Israelites as well as all other downtrodden and oppressed peoples of all lands. Here we have found a home where we can worship God in our own way."

With these words, Rabbi Shoher opened the dedication of the synagogue by serving the Jewish residents of Medway and Holliston on August 28, 1899. The Hebrew calendar places this day in the month of Eleth, the 22nd day, in the year 5659.

The ceremony had been many years in the making. The first synagogue established for Holliston and Medway was located on Hill Street. The one-story building was nearly square, with dimensions of 36 by 26 feet, and a roof, peaked in the center. At noon on the day of dedication, a procession was formed at Glatky's house, headed by a horse and carriage. A short distance behind marched the people, headed by a small band of musicians from Boston. In the center of the crowd walked one man holding the Torah.

Nine

TO PROTECT AND SERVE

The 1956 Memorial Day Parade featured the Holliston Police Department, headed by newly-appointed Chief Henry Holbrook, who marched with his daughter, Sharon, at his side.

Holliston's longest serving chief was Lewis T. Holbrook, a 35-year veteran sleuth of many local crime scenes, as well as the truancy officer. He was famous for his homespun philosophy, his dry sense of humor, and his loyalty and friendship to all the townspeople of Holliston.

Crime-fighting equipment was austere in Lewis T. Holbrook's day. He labored, often alone, day and night, had no radios for most of his years on the road, and communicated mostly by telephone. He is standing proudly by his cruiser, a familiar sight around Holliston.

Chief Lewis T. Holbrook completed his service to the town of Holliston on January 31, 1956, and passed his chief's badge on to his nephew, Henry S. Holbrook. The "police station" at that time was located in the town hall, which also housed the lockup in the far corner of the lower level. Little changed over the years of Lewis T.'s tenure, but when Henry S. Holbrook took over, many changes took place in how police work was conducted in Holliston.

One job has not changed for the police chief and the men and women who serve with him. The amount of paperwork has continued to grow, despite computers and other electronic enhancements. Paper still accumulates in the file cabinets of the department, just as 33-year-old Chief Henry S. Holbrook found out on his first day as chief.

103

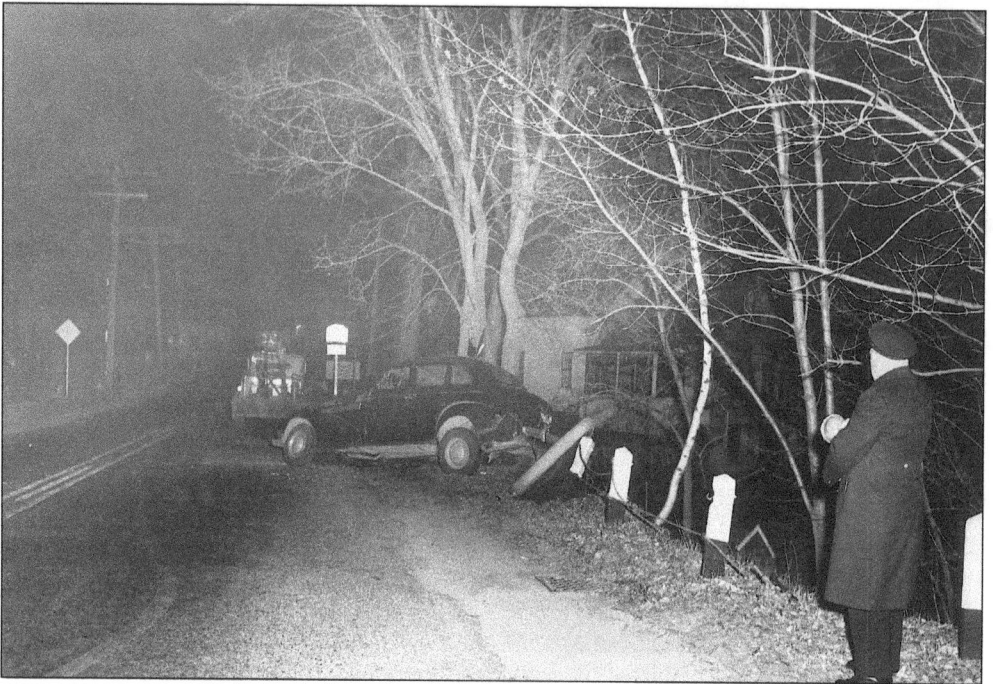

Chief Lewis T. Holbrook could be found on the job at any time of the day or night. He is presiding over an accident scene on Washington Street near Curve Street in November 1951.

Three local youths were not seriously injured in this 1954 two-car accident, at the corner of Exchange and Union Streets. Still a popular location of motor vehicle mishaps, this incident attracted a curious crowd, as Officer Ed Seariac presided over the investigation and as tow trucks began to clear up the scene.

Roads were gradually transformed from cart roads, but conditions were not optimum for motorized travel. Motor vehicle accidents were a weekly occurrence in Holliston during the early decades of the twentieth century. This spectacular scene occurred on Washington Street, near Linden Street, in November 1937. The condition of the driver was not recorded.

The Gates Garage at East Holliston was the scene of this accident during a snowstorm.

The Holliston Police Department continues to march in Memorial Day parades. The force, in 1970, carries on a proud tradition.

Hist! Hist! Hist.
The force is on the scent.
Sh! Sh! Sh!
Just see his armament:
A shot-gun and revolver,
Brass knuckles and a club.
The Holliston Police Force
Ain't No Dub!

"Holliston Night Life, A Mellow Drama"
—Anonymous, 1915

A company of the Holliston Fire Department poses for a group portrait, near their station on Central Street. Horse-drawn apparatus was used until the 1920s.

Our Firehouse clock is something new,
(The Station itself is youngish, too),
But very strange it seems to me
That such a feminine chime should be
In a red brick tower with a dreadful dome,
Like a miniature capitol strayed from home,
With nothing to hear from the world below
But the firemen snoring loud and slow,
Or a brazen clang and rattling din
When some alarm has been turned in,
While the snorers curse in a shocking way
And stumble about like fools in a play.

—Anonymous, 1931

Two fire engineers of the Holliston Fire Department pose for a formal portrait. Usually there were three men designated as engineers for the department. The whereabouts of the third man is open to speculation.

Holliston used steam engines for firefighting from 1871 until the early years of the twentieth century. The Steamer company poses in front of the old fire station on Central Street. Apparently not all members were present for this group portrait, as each company required about 40 men to operate the machine at each fire.

The Metcalf Station closed its doors in 1899. The fire apparatus kept there, the old handtub, was put into mothballs and forgotten for a half century. Fire protection would be sent from downtown for many decades to come.

The old Metcalf Fire Station, long empty and boarded up, is in this 1982 photograph. The building remains near the intersection of Washington and Summer Streets, atop the knoll once called Cat Hill.

After World War II, a group of East Holliston residents saw the need for increased fire protection and rapid response for their side of town. In 1950, they built a fire engine from war surplus parts. Other equipment and labor were acquired through their own expertise. Herbert and Clarence Gates (left) may have contributed a few spare Hudson motor parts to the vehicle. The East Holliston fire station was named in honor of Clarence Gates, for his years of dedicated service. Loring Lovewell is seen on the right.

Hydrant three, the old handtub from the Metcalf Station, lived to fight again. Restored in the early 1950s, the old tub was brought to fire musters and competitions throughout New England. Hydrant Three placed fourth with a stream of 183 feet, 9.5 inches, at Somersworth, New Hampshire, 1954.

110

Ten

GROUPS AND SOCIETIES

The Holliston Historical Society was founded in 1910, for the preservation of local history. Meetings were held at various locations around Holliston until the Burnap house was purchased in the 1920s. The house possessed its own rich history. It was the former home of Dr. Sewall Burnap, the town's physician during the Civil War era, and had provided space for the post office, which was accessed by way of the door on the left.

The Historical Society was home to many activities. Schoolchildren visited the house annually for guided tours about the history of Holliston. Members operated a dining room there for many years.

Bake sales, fairs, and auctions were popular activities at the house, as shown in this June 1963 photograph.

Time began to march on once more. The Historical Society purchased a larger property at 547 Washington Street, and moved out of the residence next to the library. The house was occupied in 1976 by Al's Restaurant, which had formerly been located in the old Hollis Hotel building at the west side of the town square.

Times changed and moved quickly. The old Burnap house was razed in 1976, and the lot was made bare in preparation for a new bank building.

The new Holliston Historical Society took up residence at 547 Washington Street during the 1970s. Here, social activities were expanded, and the buildings were often rented for weddings, parties, and business functions. The society continues its mission of preserving and enhancing the history of Holliston.

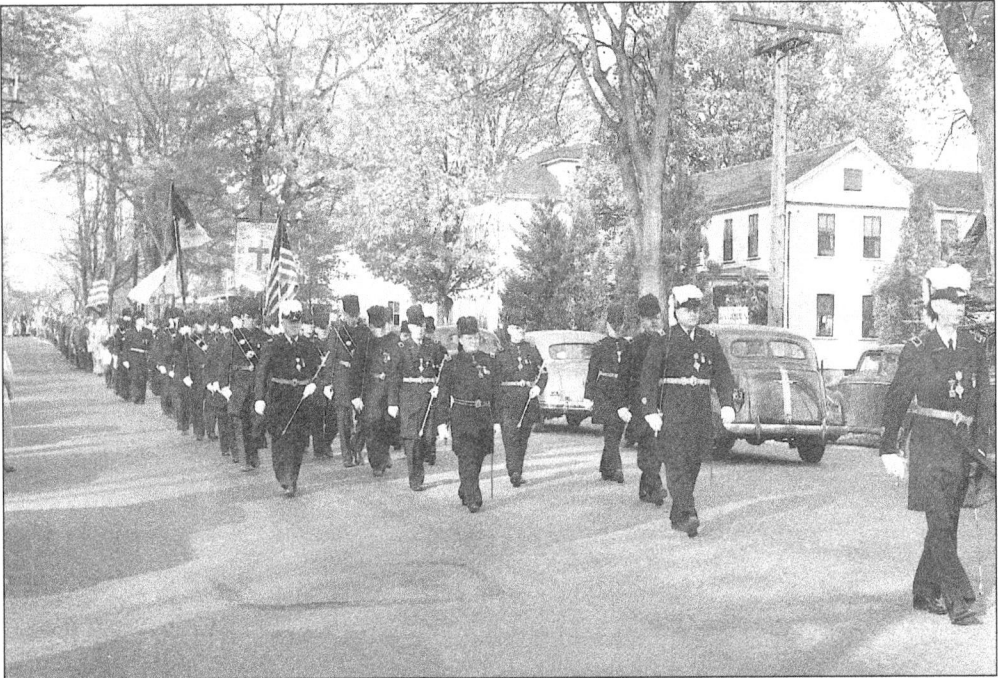

The Mount Hollis Masonic Lodge has been a strong fraternal organization for more than 100 years. The old Methodist church building at Church Place has been their headquarters since before 1950. A procession marches from their lodge to services held at the Congregational Church in 1949.

The officers of the Mount Hollis Lodge in 1949 were Edward "Doc" Holbrook, Alan Bliss, and Jimmy Inches (seated in front).

The Masquerade Ball, sponsored by the Odd Fellows and held annually at the town hall during Lent, was one of the biggest social events of the year. The portrait of the participants of a 1920s ball shows the enthusiasm of the participants and the curiosity of the more modest spectators in the balcony. Perhaps this was Holliston's substitute for the Mardi Gras!

Eleven

PARTING SHOTS

The construction of the water tower on Mount Hollis in 1890 was an engineering feat not seen before in Holliston. Townspeople marveled at the prospect of receiving clean water out of their kitchen faucets, while the construction workers marveled at the spectacular view from the top of the tower.

Lake Winthrop continued to increase in popularity for recreational activity. Having more than 10 acres of area, Winthrop is a "Great Pond," according to state standards of measurement. The lake had been known as a good place to be near since Native Americans inhabited the area, when this body of pleasant water was called "Wennakeening."

Lake Winthrop Holliston

Grape Island is on the right, and Pleasure Point is nestled among the trees in the distance. Established as a recreation area in the 1880s, the Point is the oldest beach area on Lake Winthrop. There is evidence that the Nipmuc Indians frequented this spot long before the Fair brothers saw an opportunity to establish a recreation area there.

118

The concept of a beach with a comfortable sandy stretch came later in the evolution of Pleasure Point. Most activity centered around canoeing, baseball, and campfires. Swimming in the 1890s was mostly indulged by men and boys, and several complaints were filed about their obnoxious behavior while swimming *au naturel*. When women finally joined the ranks of the swimmers, behavior improved.

The Sachem's canoe is unloosed from the shore;
It darts from a cove where are maples o'erleaning;
And the strong heart beats quick of the stalwart rower,
As it glides like a bird o'er the bright Wennakeening.

Far yonder a maiden is listening tonight;
She hears a soft ripple, she guesses its meaning;
Her cheek is suffused with a flush of delight,
As he flies to her side o'er the blue Wennakeening

from "Wennakeening"
—Anson Daniels, 1883

The Twin Elms, Holliston, Mass. 1747

The Washington Elms were important landmarks in Holliston and were mentioned often in historical annals. George Washington was said to have admired them when he passed by this way in November 1789. The two majestic trees withstood two centuries of ice, snow, hurricanes, encroaching trolley tracks, automobiles, roving hives of honeybees, and the impending doom of Dutch elm disease.

10903 The Elms, Washington St., Holliston, Mass.

Such an integral part of Holliston's identity, the towering trees were depicted on the town's postcards and were sketched, photographed, and revered as noble denizens of the forest.

The last Washington Elm finally succumbed to the saw blade in March 1951. Carl Barnes and Stanley Kurzontkowski make the final cuts before the tree toppled down.

This collection contains many photographs that reveal evidence of the trolleys that rolled through Holliston in the early years of the twentieth century. The cars traveled from Framingham to Milford, with a car barn located halfway between at East Holliston, a barn that later housed the Gates Brothers Hudson dealership and gas station.

The run of the trolleys was short-lived. Automobiles soon gained popularity, and the trolleys quickly disappeared in the 1920s. As happened so often in the early years of automotive age, many cars had a difficult time staying on the roads, as was apparent in this 1927 accident scene along Washington Street.

122

Local travelers took to the automobile with unbridled enthusiasm. This proud owner and driver is P.F. Leland, with his son as navigator, and his wife safely veiled in the back seat accompanied by daughter Dorothy.

Train service to Holliston hung on until 1959. Here, an engine exits from the "tunnel" that passes under Highland Street. The pull of the open road was too much even for these iron giants. No trains have passed through Holliston since the 1980s, when an occasional freight train visited Dennison and Axton Cross. The old railroad tunnel was unable to accommodate the larger engines and boxcars, and the arched bridge near Woodland Street made many an engineer at least a little nervous.

A birds-eye view of Washington Street, Highland Street, Phipps Hill, and Chicken Brook

wending its way southward through the trees in the foreground was taken in 1949.

For children growing up in East Holliston during the 1940s and 1950s, there was no other more important celebrity than Cinnamon, the horse owned by Clarence Gates, who resided in a paddock near the East Holliston corner. Cinnamon was sort of war surplus. An old U.S. Army cavalry horse, he spent his retirement years watching the traffic pass by and was apparently happy doing just that, as he lived to the ripe old age of 30. Cinnamon was strategically located just across Concord Street from Costa's store and was undoubtedly the major recipient of most of the candy and carrots purchased there.

Shown in a 1960 photograph, Outpost Farm, founded by Charlie Nickerson, fast became a landmark in Holliston and a mecca for buyers of Thanksgiving Day turkeys, as well as pies, produce, and preserves for every day of the year.

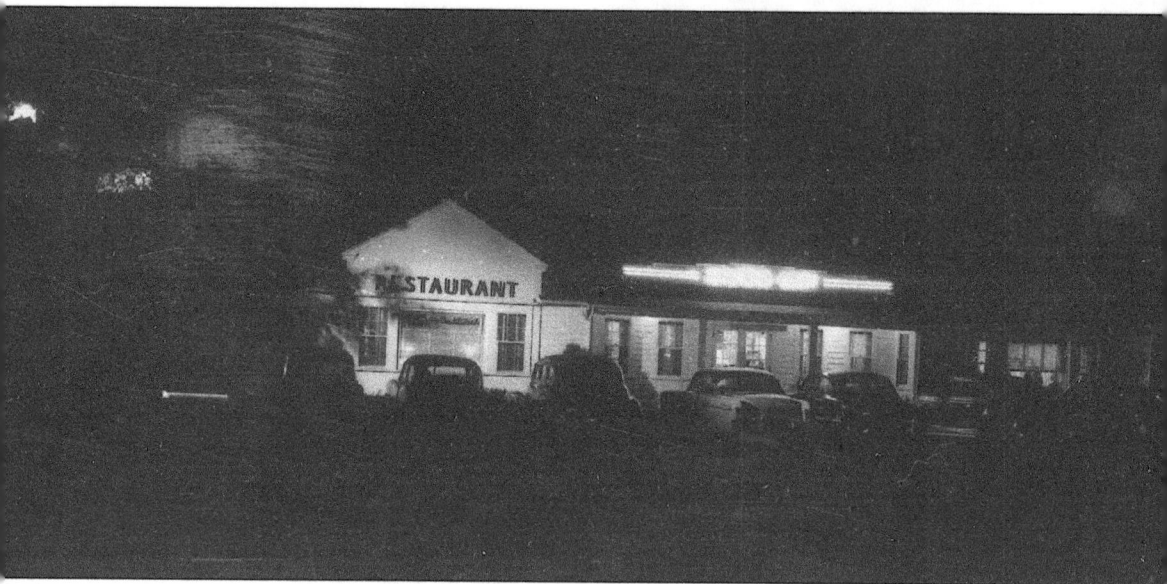

An important chapter in the town's history ended when Walter's Dairy closed its doors. Holliston's most famous night spot passed on as cherished memories for all those who worked there, stopped by for dinner or ice cream, or met out in the parking lot. No other spot has ever taken its place in the minds and hearts of Holliston, and so it provides a fitting end to this second volume of photographs about the town of Holliston.

www.ingramcontent.com/pod-product-compliance
Lightning Source LLC
Chambersburg PA
CBHW080858100426
42812CB00007B/2075